SCHIRMER
PERFORMANCE
EDITIONS

BEETHOVEN

SONATA in C Minor
Opus 13 ("Pathétique")

Edited and Recorded by Robert Taub

T0087640

To access companion recorded performances online, visit:
www.halleonard.com/mylibrary

Enter Code
4376-7493-7335-3472

On the cover:
A Mountain Peak with Drifting Clouds

by Casper David Friedrich
(ca. 1835)

© Kimbell Art Museum/CORBIS

ISBN: 978-1-4234-2722-3

G. SCHIRMER, Inc.

DISTRIBUTED BY

HAL•LEONARD®
CORPORATION

7777 W. BLUEMOUND RD. P.O. BOX 13819 MILWAUKEE, WI 53213

www. musicsalesclassical.com
www.halleonard.com

CONTENTS

Sonata in C minor, Opus 13 ("Pathétique")
First movement
Grave [♪ = 60]

Second movement
Adagio cantabile [♪ = 66]

Third movement
Rondo
Allegro [♩ = 84]

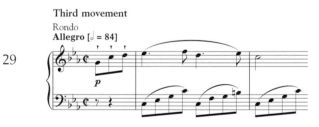

The price of this publication includes access to companion recorded performances online, for download or streaming, using the unique code found on the title page.
Visit **www.halleonard.com/mylibrary** and enter the access code.

HISTORICAL NOTES

LUDWIG VAN BEETHOVEN (1770-1827)

THE PIANO SONATAS

In 1816, Beethoven wrote to his friend and admirer Carl Czerny: "You must forgive a composer who would rather hear his work just as he had written it, however beautifully you played it otherwise." Having lost patience with Czerny's excessive interpolations in the piano part of a performance of Beethoven's *Quintet for Piano and Winds*, Op. 16, Beethoven also addressed the envelope sarcastically to "Herr von Zerni, celebrated virtuoso." On all levels, Beethoven meant what he wrote.

As a composer who bridged the gulf between court and private patronage on one hand (the world of Bach, Handel, Haydn, and Mozart) and on the other hand earning a living based substantially on sales of printed works and/or public perform-ances (the world of Brahms), Beethoven was one of the first composers to became almost obsessively concerned with the accuracy of his published scores. He often bemoaned the seeming unending streams of mistakes. "Fehler—fehler!—Sie sind selbst ein einziger Fehler" ("Mistakes—mistakes!—You yourselves are a unique mistake") he wrote to the august publishing firm of Breitkopf und Härtel in 1811.

It is not surprising, therefore, that toward the end of his life Beethoven twice (1822 and again in 1825) begged his publishers C.F. Peters and Schott to bring out a comprehensive complete edition of his works over which Beethoven himself would have editorial control, and would thus be able to ensure accuracy in all dimen-sions—notes, pedaling and fingering, expressive notations (dynamics, slurs), and articulations, and even movement headings. This never happened.

Beethoven was also obsessive about his musical sketches that he kept with him throughout his mature life. Desk sketchbooks, pocket sketchbooks: thousands of pages reveal his innermost compositional musings, his labored processes of creativity, the ideas that he abandoned, and the many others—often jumbled together—that he crafted through dint of extraordinary determination, single-minded purpose, and the inspiration of genius into works that endure all exigencies of time and place. In the autograph scores that Beethoven then sent on to pub-lishers, further layers of the creative processes abound. But even these scores might not be the final word in a particular work; there are instances in which Beethoven made textual changes, additions, or deletions by way of letters to publishers, corrections to proofs, and/or post-publication changes to first editions.

We can appreciate the unique qualities of the Beethoven piano sonatas on many different levels. Beethoven's own relationship with these works was fundamentally different from his relationship to his works of other genres. The early sonatas served as vehicles for the young Beethoven as both composer and pianist forging his path in Vienna, the musical capital of Europe at that time. Throughout his compositional lifetime, even when he no longer performed publicly as a pianist, Beethoven used his 32 piano sonatas as crucibles for all manner of musical ideas, many of which he later re-crafted—often in a distilled or more rarefied manner—in the 16 string quartets and the nine symphonies.

The pianoforte was evolving at an enormous rate during the last years of the 18th century extending through first several decades of the 19th. As a leading pianist and musical figure of his day, Beethoven was in the vanguard of this technological development. He was not content to confine his often explosive playing to the smaller sonorous capabilities of the instruments he had on hand; similarly, his compositions demanded more from the pianofortes of the day—greater depth of sonority, more subtle levels of keyboard finesse and control, increased registral range. These sonatas themselves pushed forward further development and technical innovation from the piano manufacturers.

Motivating many of the sonatas are elements of extraordinary—even revolutionary—musical experimentation extending into domains of form, harmonic development, use of the instrument, and demands placed upon the performer, the piano, and the audience. However, the evolution of these works is not a simple straight line.

I believe that the usual chronological groupings of "early," "middle," and "late" are too superficial for Beethoven's piano sonatas. Since he composed more piano sonatas than substantial works of any other single genre (except songs) and the period of composition of the piano sonatas extends virtually throughout Beethoven's entire creative life, I prefer chronological groupings derived from more specific biographical and stylistic considerations. I delve into greater depth on this and other aspects of the Sonatas in my book *Playing the Beethoven Piano Sonatas* (Amadeus Press).

1795-1800: Sonatas Op. 2 no. 1, Op. 2 no. 2, Op. 2 no. 3, Op. 7, Op. 10 no. 1, Op. 10 no. 2, Op. 10 no. 3, Op. 13, Op. 14 no. 1, Op. 14 no. 2, Op. 22, Op. 49 no. 1, Op. 49 no. 2

1800-1802: Sonatas Op. 27 no. 1, Op. 27 no. 2, Op. 28, Op. 31 no. 1, Op. 31 no. 2, Op. 31 no. 3

1804: Sonatas Op. 53, Op. 54, Op. 57

1809: Sonatas Op. 78, Op. 79, Op. 81a

1816-1822: Sonatas Op. 90, Op. 101, Op. 106, Op. 109, Op. 110, Op. 111

From 1804 (post-Heiligenstadt) forward, there were no more multiple sonata opus numbers; each work was assigned its own opus. Beethoven no longer played in public, and his relationship with the sonatas changed subtly.

—*Robert Taub*

PERFORMANCE NOTES

For the preparation of this edition, I have consulted autograph scores, first editions, and sketchbooks whenever possible. (Complete autograph scores of only 12 of the piano sonatas—plus the autograph of only the first movement of Sonata Op. 81a—have survived.) I have also read Beethoven's letters with particular attention to his many remarks concerning performances of his day and the lists of specific changes/corrections that he sent to publishers. We all know—as did Beethoven—that musical notation is imperfect, but it is the closest representation that we have of the artistic ideal of a composer. We strive to represent that ideal as thoroughly and accurately as possible.

General Observations

Tempo

My recording of this sonata is included in the published volume. I have also included my suggestions for tempo (metronome markings) at the beginning of each movement.

Fingering

I have added my own fingering suggestions, all of which are aimed at creating meaningful musical constructs. As a general guide, I believe in minimizing hand motions as much as possible, and therefore many of my fingering suggestions are based on the pianist's hands proceeding in a straight line as long as musically viable and physically practicable. I also believe that the pianist can develop senses of tactile feeling for specific musical patterns.

Pedaling

Beethoven did not include pedal markings for this sonata. However, whenever necessary one should use the right pedal—sparingly and subtly—to help achieve legato playing as well as to enhance sonorities.

Ornamentation

My suggestions regarding ornamental turns concern the notion of keeping the contour smooth while providing an expressive musical gesture with an increased sense of forward direction. The actual starting note of a turn depends on the specific context: if it is preceded by the same note (as in Sonata Op. 10 no. 2, second movement, m. 42), then I would suggest that the turn is four notes, starting on the upper neighbor: upper neighbor, main note, lower neighbor, main note.

Sonata in F Major, Op. 10 no. 2:
second movement, m. 42

However, if the turn is preceded by another note (as in Sonata Op. 10 no. 2, first movement, m. 38), then the turn could be five notes in total, starting on the main note: main note, upper neighbor, main note, lower neighbor, main note.

Sonata in F Major, Op. 10 no. 2:
first movement, m. 38

Whenever Beethoven included an afterbeat (Nachschlag) for a trill, I have included it as well. When he did not, I have not added any.

About the Edition

Footnotes within the musical score offer contextual explanations and alternatives based on earlier representations of the music (first editions, autograph scores) that Beethoven had seen and corrected. In specific cases that are visible only in the autograph score, I explain the reasons and context for my choices of musical representation. Other footnotes are intended to clarify ways of playing specific ornaments.

Above all, Beethoven's sonatas—as individual works, or taken together as a complete cycle—are pieces that we can listen to, learn, play, put away, re-learn, and perform again over and over—with only increasing joy, involvement, and meaning. For those of you looking at the musical score as you follow a recording, welcome. For those playing this piece for the first time, I invite you to become involved. And for those returning to this sonata after learning it previously—or comparing this edition to any other—I invite you to roll up your sleeves and start playing, for there is always more to do.

The expressive universe conjured up by the Beethoven piano sonatas is unprecedented, and unequalled.

Notes on the Sonata*

Sonata in C minor, Opus 13 ("Pathétique") (1798-99)

First Movement: Grave—Allegro molto e con brio

That Beethoven himself designated the sobriquet "Pathétique" for this sonata indicates that he fully intended for others to appreciate its dramatic content. C minor was Beethoven's Sturm und Drang key. His three piano sonatas in C minor—Op. 10 no. 1, Op. 13, and Op. 111—are all infused with extraordinary intensity. It is unique that Beethoven should use the same key (C minor) for

two sonatas, Op. 10 no. 1 and Op. 13, that were composed so closely together. Sonata Op. 10 no. 1 is concentrated and concise. Sonata Op. 13, composed less than two years afterward, uses the same key scheme for its three movements (C minor, A-flat major, C minor) but is more expansive in conception. The Grave as slow music *before* the Allegro is unique in the canon of Beethoven sonatas published by that time, but Beethoven himself actually experimented with a similar concept of integrating slow dramatic phrases within the framework of an *allegro* first movement in his Sonata in F minor, WoO 47 that he composed in Bonn as a young man of 13. Beethoven was likely also familiar with a Dussek piano work of 1793 in C minor entitled *The Sufferings of the Queen of France, A Musical Composition Expressing the feelings of the Unfortunate Marie Antoinette During her Imprisonment, Trial, Etc.* This work also begins with a slow introduction and consists of ten descriptive sections, more along the lines of a fantasy.

Fp is the first marking of Op. 13: what does it mean? how is it played? The idea is for the chord to be heard *forte* initially, then rapidly dying down to *piano*. This is fundamentally different from an accent within a *piano* context and from the *sforzando* marking first encountered here in m. 4. Beethoven could also have notated the first chord as *forte* and then placed a *piano* marking under the second chord, implying that the dynamic level naturally decays from *forte* to *piano*. To achieve an effective *fp*, the pianist simply depresses the keys rapidly, creating the *forte*, then immediately allows them to rise so that the sound is damped almost instantaneously. Depressing the keys immediately once again so that the dampers rise quickly allows the strings to continue to vibrate but now with considerably less energy, *piano*. All this takes only a small fraction of a second but sets the stage for the drama that unfolds throughout the piece.

*Excerpted from *Playing the Beethoven Piano Sonatas* by Robert Taub
© 2002 by Robert Taub
Published by Amadeus Press
Used by permission.

The tempo of the Grave is slow enough so that the 64th note groupings (and also the 128th-notes) are clear but not so slow as to be ponderous. Dynamic contrasts and long rests are integral to the drama. The Allegro molto enters without interruption, and here, since the harmonic motion is basically slow, I play at the fastest tempo that allows for the bass tremolandos—which add mightily to the overall tension of the movement—to be transparent with only subtle pedaling. I try to resist the temptation to make a crescendo in mm. 11-14 as the right-hand line rises, and find that although the *piano* dynamic of m. 11 lasts until the crescendo in m. 15, a slight shaping upward of the line is inevitable, such is the forward momentum of the music. But keeping these measures generally soft does in fact add to the agitation and drama. The touch on the staccato half-notes (m. 15) is light, and the chords are separated but not sharply detached. I do not see any reason to slow down for the second theme (m. 51 on) but rather use a more singing tone and legato qualities of touch. I play all the mordents (m. 57 on) starting with the main note, on the beat.

Although the repeat of the exposition in the first movement of the F minor Sonata WoO47 includes a rehearing of the opening slow music, that of Sonata Op. 13 does not. The repeat sign at the end of the exposition takes us back to m. 11, the beginning of the Allegro molto. But following the rehearing of the exposition, four measures of the music of the Grave do in fact return, and the initial effect is startling: since the slow music returns here, no longer can we consider the Grave merely as introductory, and we are left wondering what is going to happen next. Portentous, weighty chords lead from the home key of C minor to E minor, rather than the dominant (G minor) which would be more expected. As the Allegro molto reenters in m. 137, we realize that we have been ushered into the development area. Crescendos that were withheld from the ascending right-hand line in the exposition are present and give the impression that the line is pushing forward even though the tempo remains steady. For the first time the left hand has the melodic fragments under right-hand tremolandos (beginning in m. 149) which should remain vibrant as they descend chromatically, leading eventually to the long-awaited dominant (m. 167). Here the tremolandos are back in the left hand, and the feeling is an unsettling combination of G major within a larger framework of C minor.

There is a story behind the repeat sign in m. 11 of the first movement. The first editions—Eder (1799) and Hoffmeister (later the same year)—both place the repeat sign in m. 11, as do all responsible modern editions. In a reprint of Op. 13 done by Haslinger (1828), the repeat sign in m. 11 is missing. It is also missing in the first complete works edition (Breitkopf und Härtel, 1864-67), but that edition is widely recognized today as containing many inaccuracies. I consider this to be an error of omission rather than an indication to begin the repetition of the exposition in m. 1, since the early editions brought out during Beethoven's lifetime have the repeat sign in the same place (m. 11) and there is no correspondence from Beethoven about changing it.

Just to be sure, I have tried playing the piece both ways. I find that going back to m. 11 heightens the surprise, contrast, and drama in the recurrences of the slow music after the exposition is complete and later in the movement. But repeating the exposition from m. 1—and therefore hearing the entire Grave twice—lessens the impact of these recurrences.

Unlike the earlier F minor sonata, the recapitulation of which is more literal and includes the slow music from the opening, the recapitulation here does not include music from the opening Grave. But the coda does. Beginning in m. 295 the *fp* chords are replaced by rests; three groups of dotted-rhythm chords ascend with increasing tension to the longest smoothly descending—and poignant—line of the movement (D-flat down an entire octave—mm. 297-298) which sets up the final reiteration of the main theme of the Allegro molto. The ensuing crescendo, once again delayed until after the right-hand ascending chords, leads to the final definitive cadence.

Second Movement: Adagio cantabile

After the contrasts of tempo of the first movement and its interruptions of phrases, its staccato notes, and its inner tension, the long, singing phrases of the second movement appear as welcome comfort. The Adagio cantabile is unabashedly lyrical with a three-tiered texture. The undulating inner accompaniment gently leads the motion forward, with the bass as a solid harmonic grounding and the top line soaring lyrically above. Each line requires a different quality of sound, a different touch—flat fingers playing lightly for an accompaniment touch; slightly heavier, more rounded fingers for a singing tone. I believe that shaping the dynamic contour of the line as it rises and falls is natural; the *piano* indication simply sets the general dynamic level. The slurs guard against overly square phrasing by suggesting more or less weight on their beginnings and ends, which are occasionally drawn where one might not usually expect to find them.

Each of the two episodes calls forth a different musical character. The stillness of the repeated bass and questioning character of the top line of the first contrast with the introspective conversant qualities of the second. When the theme returns for the last time (m. 51) the accompaniment continues the triplet motion begun in the second episode, but it is important not to push the tempo ahead at this point and to maintain the repose of the character of the theme. Beethoven is specific about the apex of the crescendos in m. 67 and m. 69: the A-flat in the right hand is the loudest point, after which the line recedes. Although the top note (A-flat) remains the same for the last three chords, the bass descends an octave, and additional pitches in the right hand complete the tonic triad. Without sacrificing the top note, I like to voice the right-hand chords to bring the descending E-flat–C to the surface subtly while the bass A-flat rings softly beneath. This iteration of the home triad as the voices accrue over the last measure allows the last chord (surprisingly without an E-flat) to resonate deeply and peacefully.

Third Movement: Rondo: Allegro

An interpretive decision for the last movement concerns its fundamental character. Is it tempestuous and headlong like the first movement, or is it more restrained, more held back? I believe the latter is the case. The only marking is Rondo: Allegro; there is no *molto* or *con brio* as there is for the first movement. The harmonic and metrical stability of the bass eighth-notes—as opposed to the tension inherent in the bass tremolandos of the first movement—adds to the resolute nature of the theme. Although this movement is alla breve, I play it less fast than the first, at a speed that allows the lyricism of the top line to be felt in all its poignancy. Noting that the main theme is a reinterpretation of the second theme of the first movement could suggest that one might play the C minor statement of the second theme with just a little more import than previous statements.

Sonata in C minor, Op. 13:
first movement, mm. 237-241

Sonata in C minor, Op. 13: third movement, mm. 1-2

The G–C–D–E-flat from the first movement form the beginning of the main theme of the last movement.

To preserve the tempo and to establish inner strength where the triplets begin (m. 33), I find a pulse of four beats per bar—rather than simply two—is helpful. Openness of tone—even within a dynamic of *piano*—is generally the rule in major key areas such as m. 44, in contrast to the soft intensity of the C minor theme. Following alternations of character between the two statements of the main theme and two major-key episodes, the primary intensity is distilled to a single chromatic descending line beginning in m. 167 before the final, most poignant statement of the theme. The bass line continues in groups of four eighth-notes in m. 179 rather than breaking with this pattern as in all previous thematic statements. This continuity, along with the right-hand eighth-notes and the crescendo, imbues the music with even greater urgency, sending it forward into the coda. Toward the end, the previous two movements are briefly recalled: mm. 203-206 are briefly in A-flat major, reminiscent in register and texture of the Adagio cantabile, and mm. 207-208 recall the first movement with its upward motion to augmented sixth and $^6_4$ harmonies of C minor. The last measures bring us back to the last movement, for the cascading triplet figure was heard twice before. But a C minor cadence is attained only with this final flourish.

A brief story about the "Pathétique" illustrates the polar extremes of response that it generated. In his introduction to the English edition of Schindler's *The Life of Beethoven*, the trustworthy pianist and composer Ignaz Moscheles (1794-1870) relates that as a young boy, he had been placed under the tutelage of Dionysius Weber, the director of the Prague Music Conservatory. Moscheles

> leanrt from some school-fellows that a young composer had appeared in Vienna, who wrote the oddest stuff possible—such as no one could either play or understand; crazy music, in opposition to all rule; and that this curiosity as to this so-called eccentric genius, I found there Beethoven's *Sonata pathétique*. This was in the year 1804. My pocket-money would not suffice for the purchase of it, so I secretly copied it. The novelty of its style was so attractive to me, and I became so enthusiastic in my admiration of it, that I forgot myself so as to mention my new acquisition to my master, who reminded me of his injunction [to study no composers other than Bach, Mozart, and Clementi for three years], and warned me not to play or study and eccentric productions until I had based my style upon more solid models. Without, however, minding his injunctions I seized upon the pianoforte works of Beethoven as they successively appeared, and in them found a solace and a delight such as no other composer afforded me.[1]

Although Sonata Op. 13 was an immediate public success, it did indeed engender criticism from conservatives. But Beethoven seemed not to be concerned with adverse responses. "Let them talk," he wrote in a letter to the publisher Hoffmeister under the date "15 January (or thereabouts) 1801": "By means of their chatter they will certainly never make anyone immortal, nor will they ever take immortality from anyone upon whom Apollo has bestowed it."[2] Beethoven could undoubtedly have continued producing works affecting in the same manner as the Sonata "Pathétique," easily amassing adulation and wealth, but the path he chose instead is revealing about his artistic motivation: having successfully composed such a work, he moved on to other musical challenges.

—Robert Taub

Footnotes

1. Alexander Wheelock Thayer, *Thayer's Life of Beethoven* (Princeton: Princeton University Press, 1973), 242-243.

2. Emily Anderson, *The Letters of Beethoven* (New York: St. Martin's Press; London: Macmillan, 1961), 48.

Dedicated to Prince Carl von Lichnowsky

Sonata in C minor

(Pathétique)

Ludwig van Beethoven
Opus 13

Grave [♪ = 60]

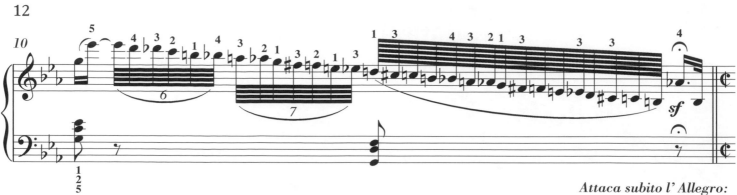

Attaca subito l' Allegro:

Allegro molto e con brio [♩ = 152]

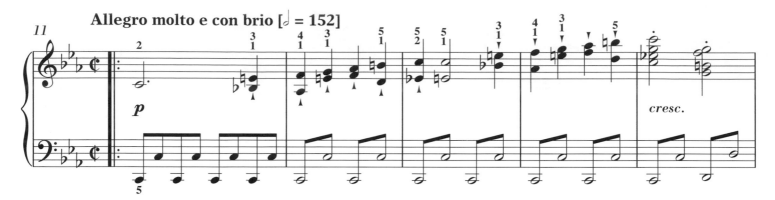

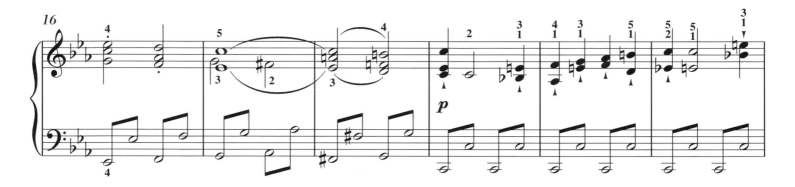

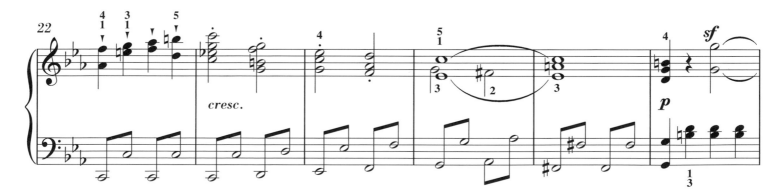

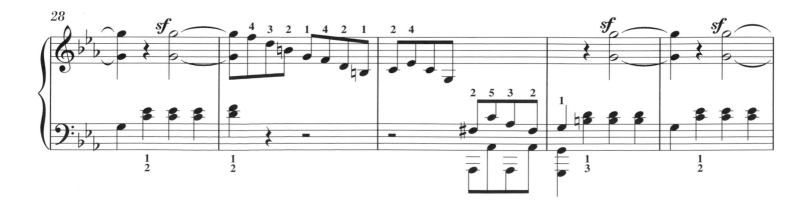

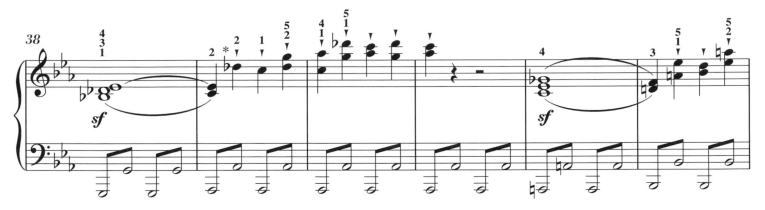

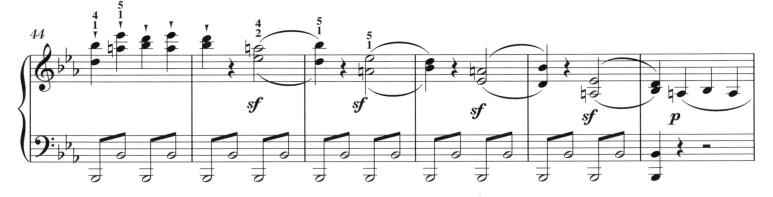

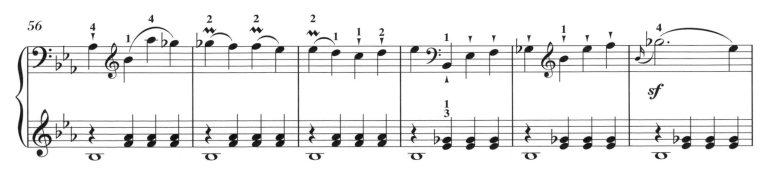

*as in the First Edition; subsequent editions have
**LH over RH
***short appoggiatura

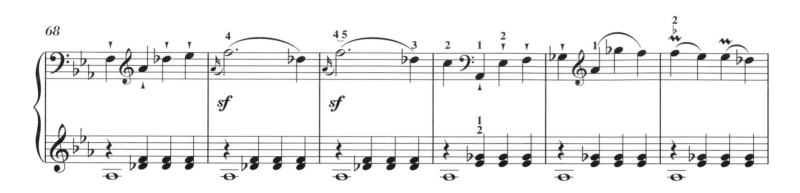

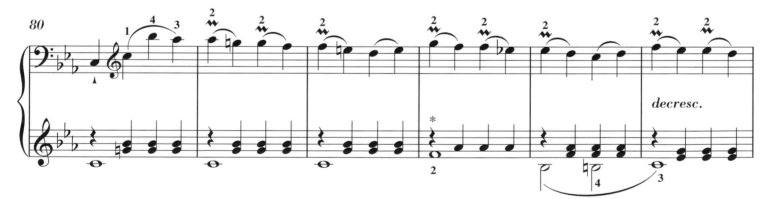

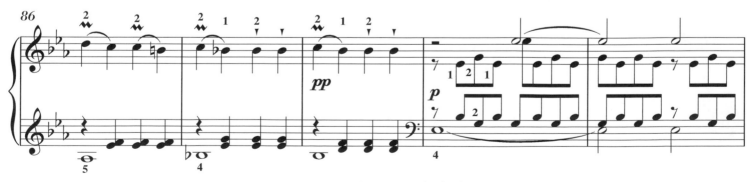

*as in the First Edition; subsequent editions have

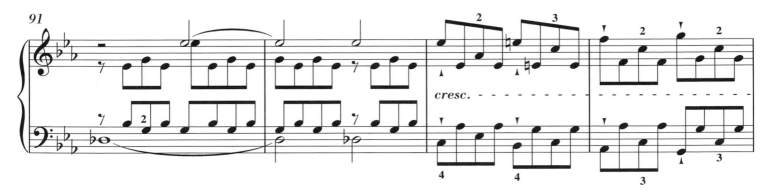

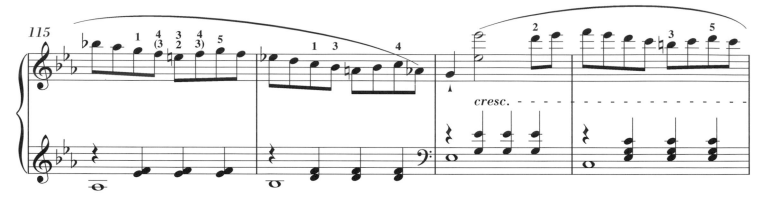

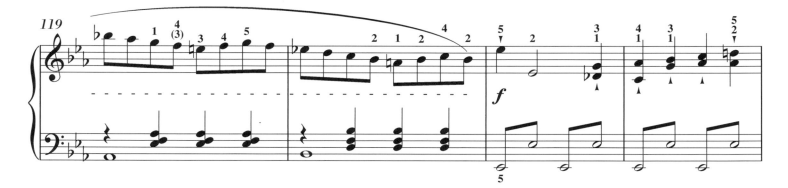

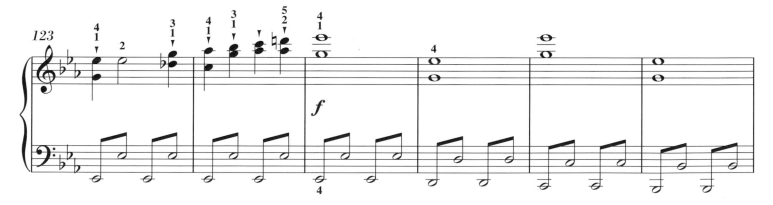

Allegro molto e con brio

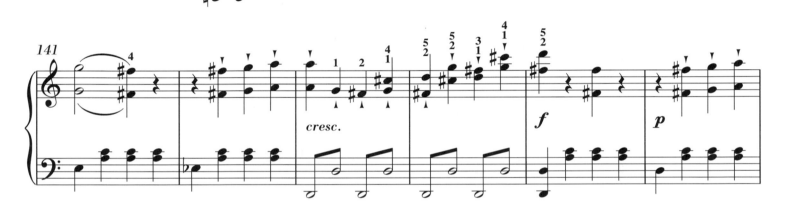

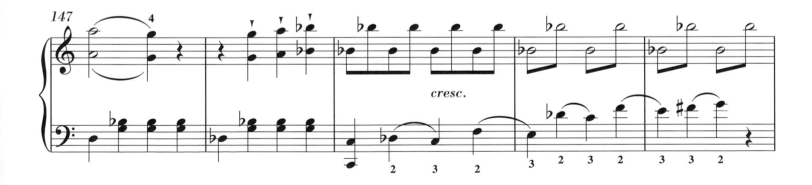

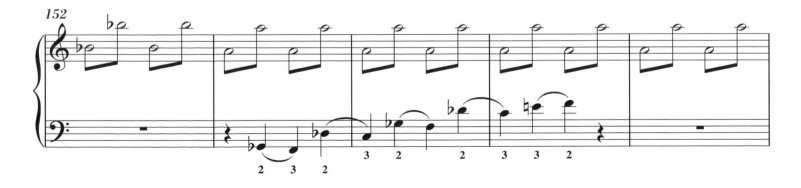

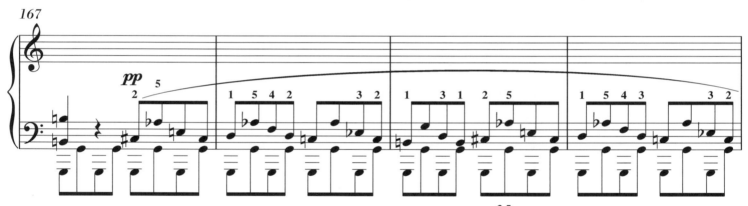

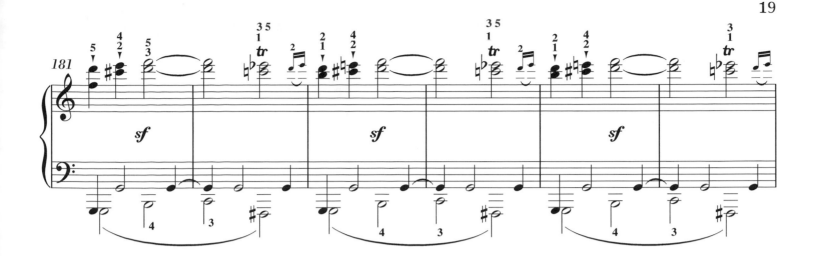

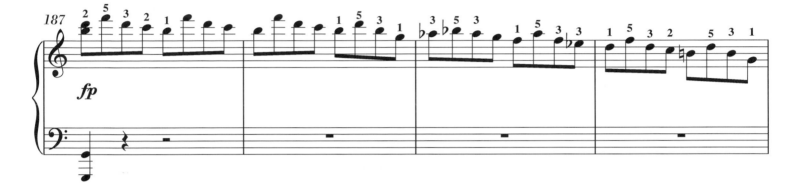

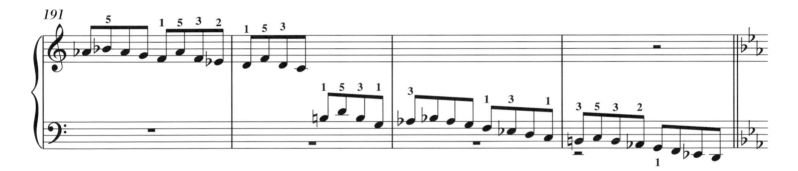

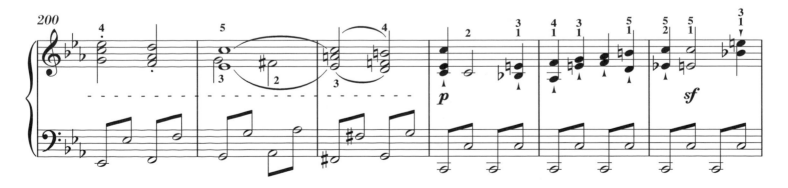

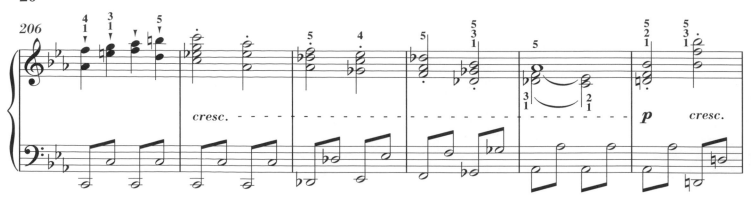

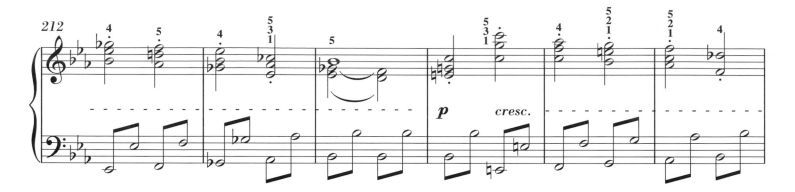

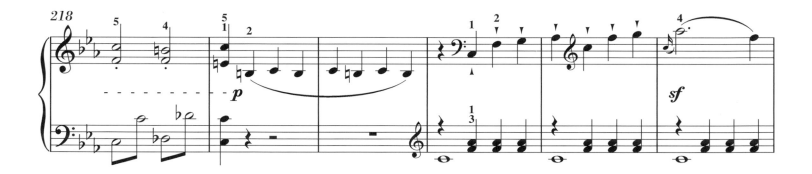

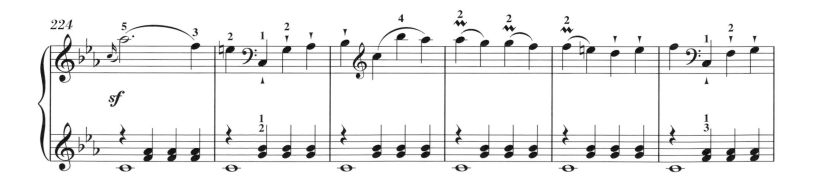

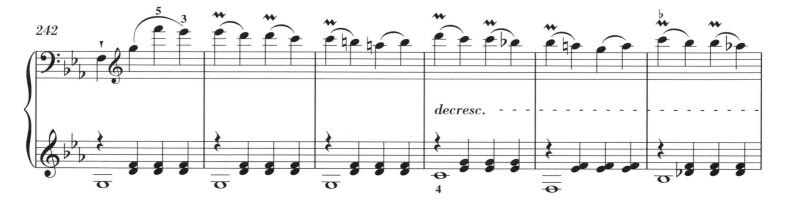

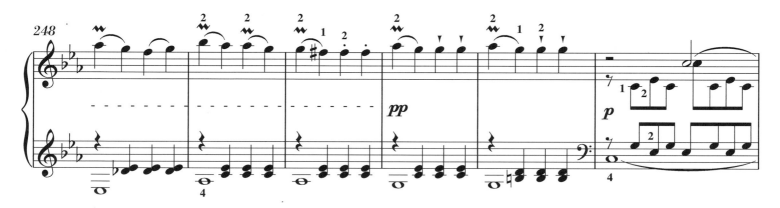

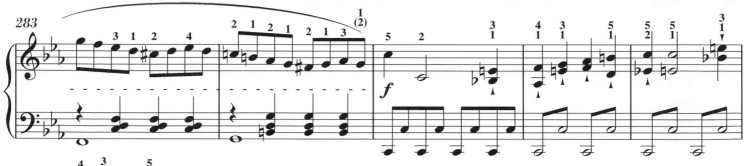

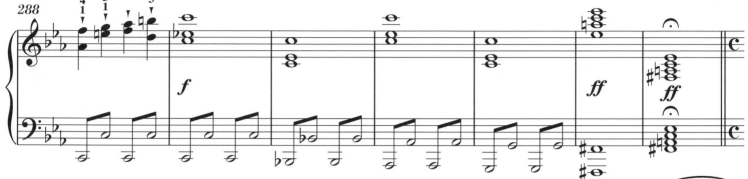

Grave

Allegro molto e con brio

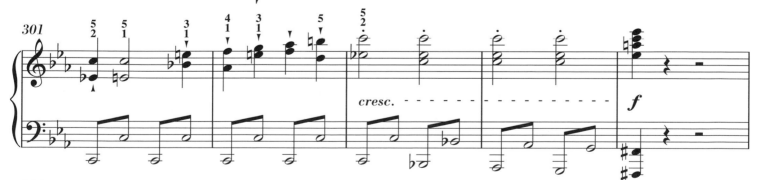

Adagio cantabile [♪ = 66]

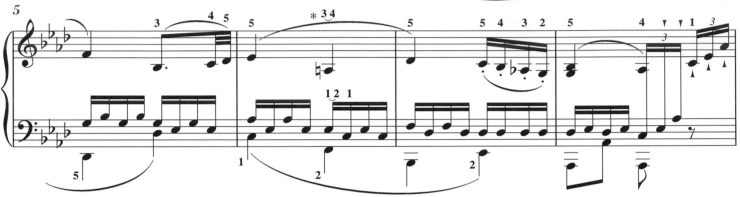

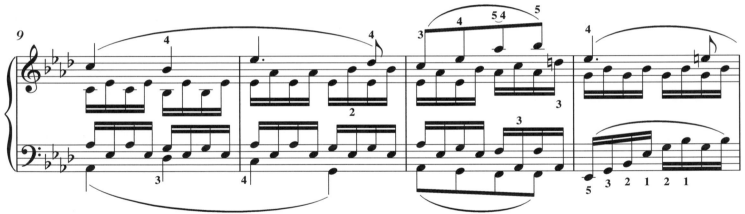

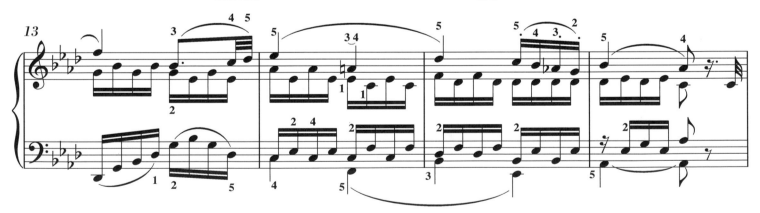

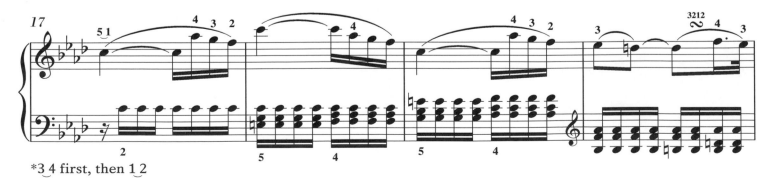

*3 4 first, then 1 2

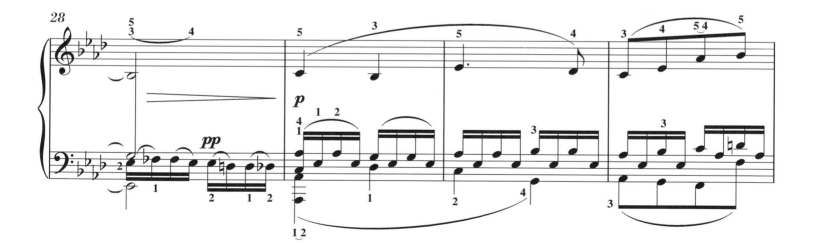

*Following the cresc. in m. 24, a drop to **mp** (subito) in m. 25.

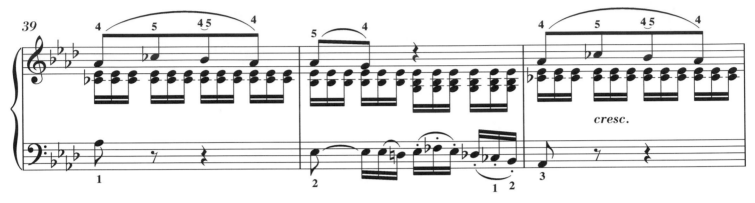

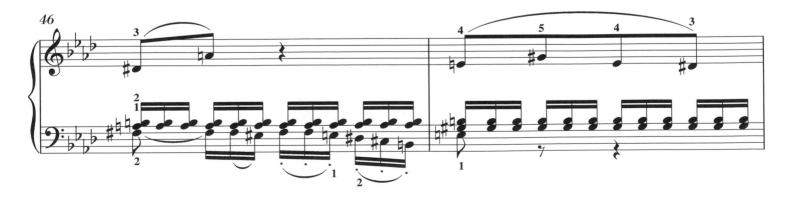

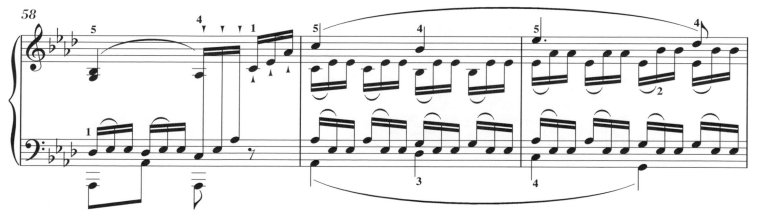

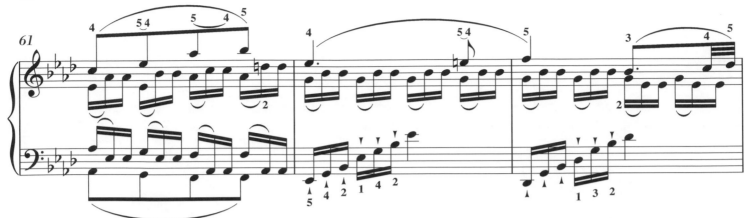

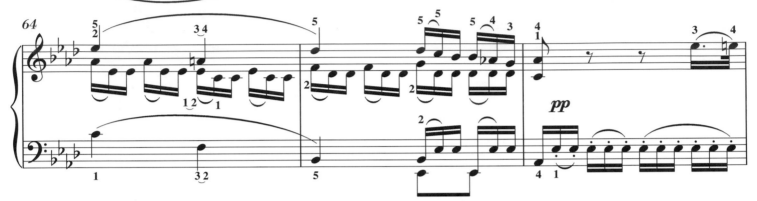

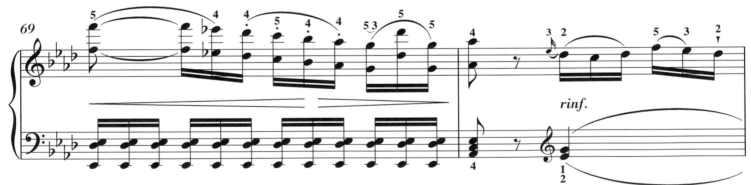

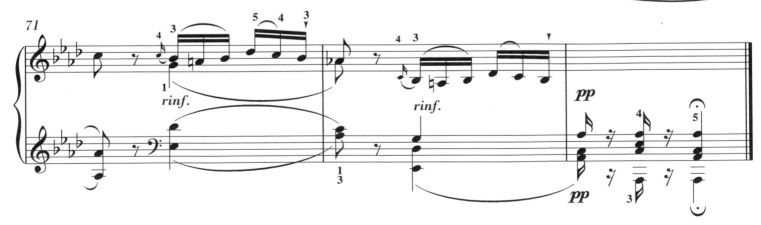

Rondo
Allegro [♩ = 84]

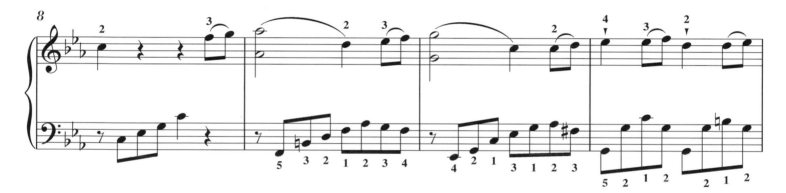

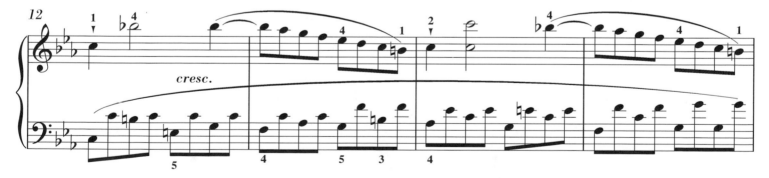

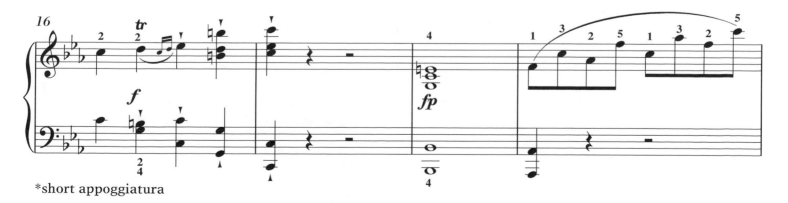

*short appoggiatura

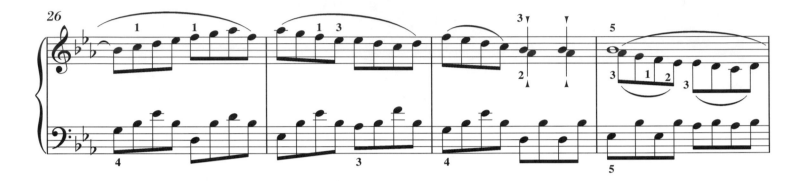

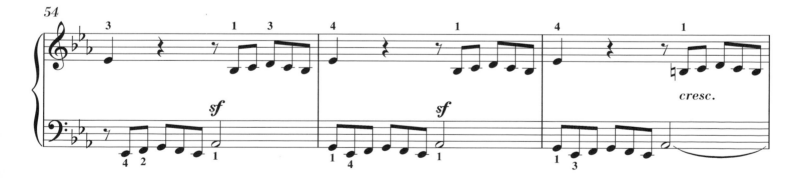

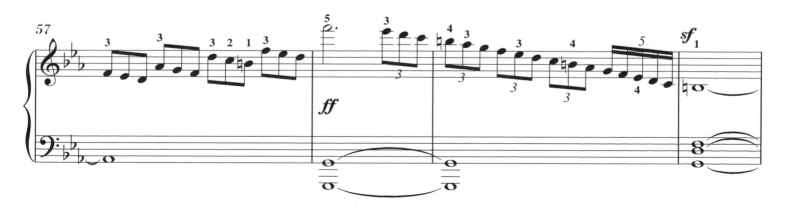

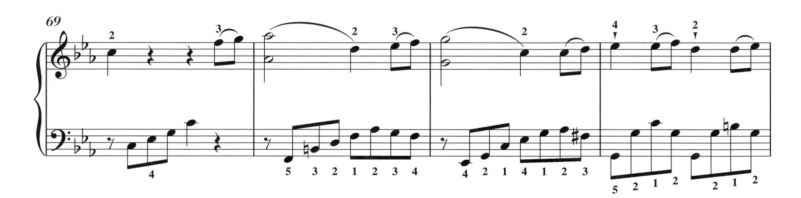

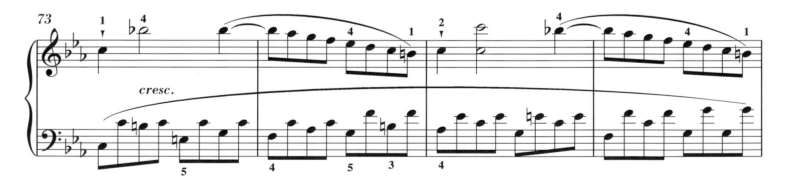

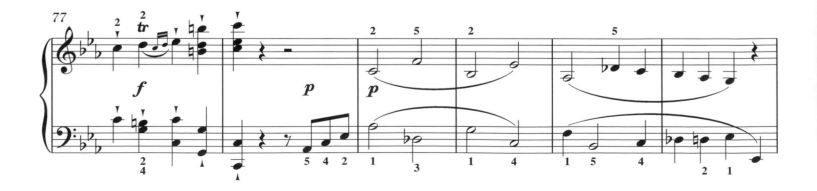

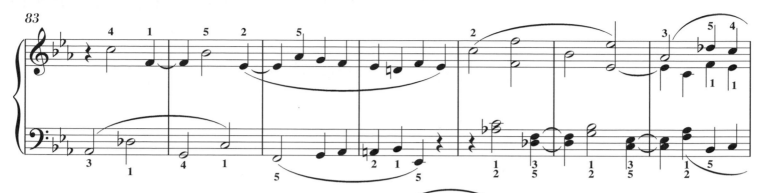

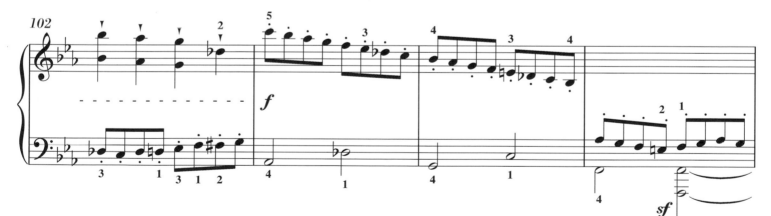

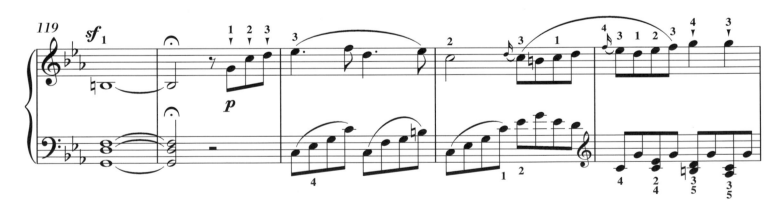

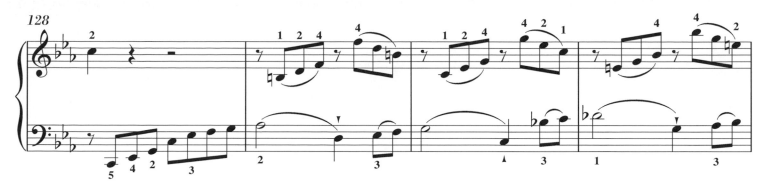

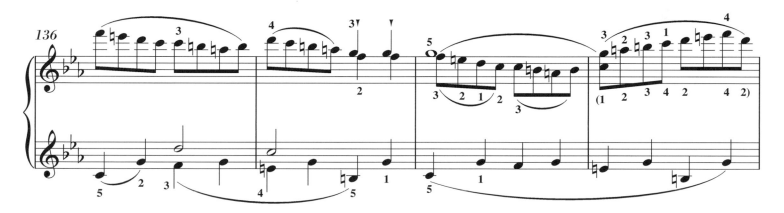

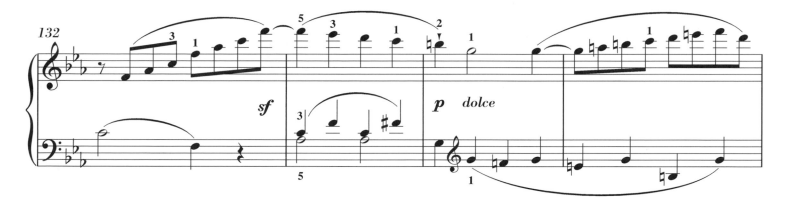

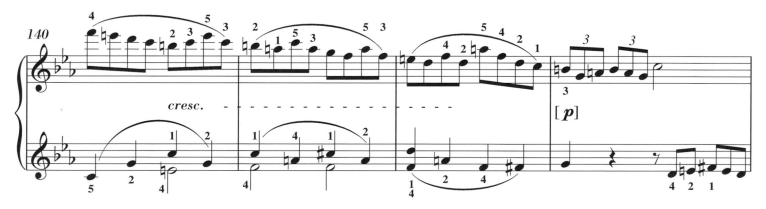

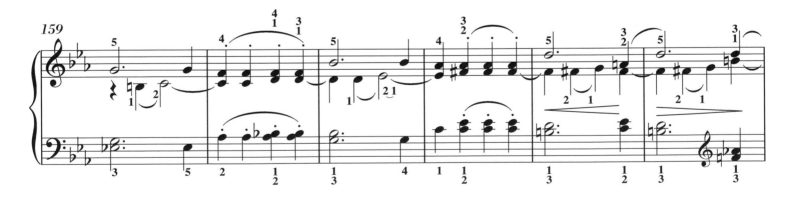

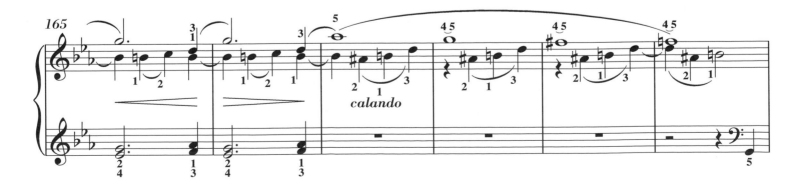

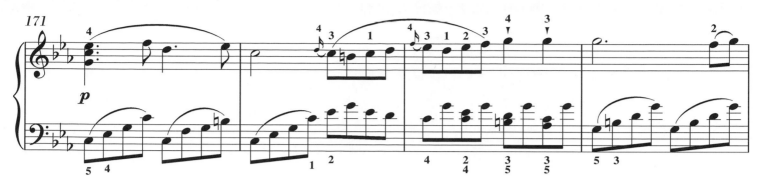

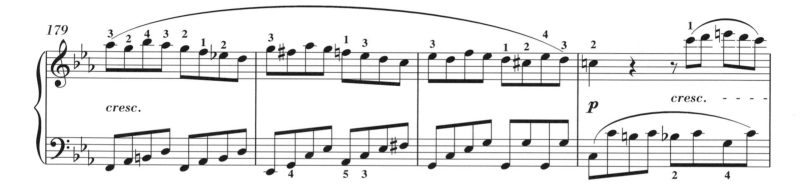

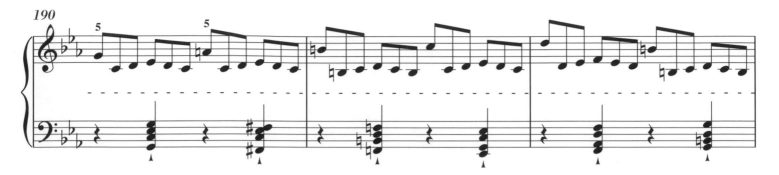

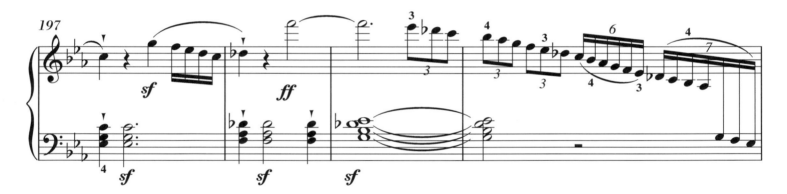

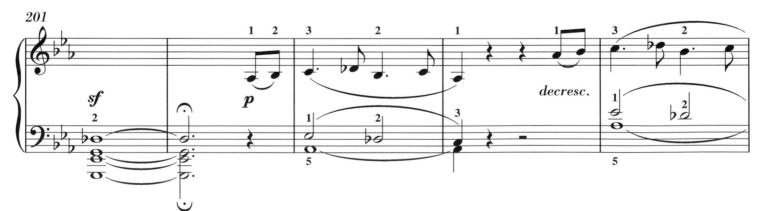

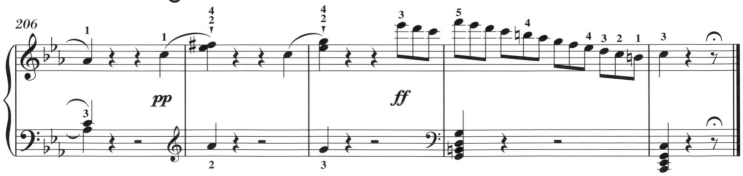

ABOUT THE EDITOR

ROBERT TAUB

From New York's Carnegie Hall to Hong Kong's Cultural Centre to Germany's *avant garde* Zentrum für Kunst und Medientechnologie, Robert Taub is acclaimed internationally. He has performed as soloist with the MET Orchestra in Carnegie Hall, the Boston Symphony Orchestra, BBC Philharmonic, The Philadelphia Orchestra, San Francisco Symphony, Los Angeles Philharmonic, Montreal Symphony, Munich Philharmonic, Orchestra of St. Luke's, Hong Kong Philharmonic, Singapore Symphony, and others.

Robert Taub has performed solo recitals on the Great Performers Series at New York's Lincoln Center and other major series worldwide. He has been featured in international festivals, including the Saratoga Festival, the Lichfield Festival in England, San Francisco's Midsummer Mozart Festival, the Geneva International Summer Festival, among others.

Following the conclusion of his highly celebrated New York series of Beethoven Piano Sonatas, Taub completed a sold-out Beethoven cycle in London at Hampton Court Palace. His recordings of the complete Beethoven Piano Sonatas have been praised throughout the world for their insight, freshness, and emotional involvement. In addition to performing, Robert Taub is an eloquent spokesman for music, giving frequent engaging and informal lectures and pre-concert talks. His book on Beethoven—*Playing the Beethoven Piano Sonatas*—has been published internationally by Amadeus Press.

Taub was featured in a 2003 PBS television program—*Big Ideas*—that highlighted him playing and discussing Beethoven Piano Sonatas. Filmed during his time as Artist-in-Residence at the Institute for Advanced Study, this program has been broadcast throughout the US on PBS affiliates.

Robert Taub's performances are frequently broadcast on radio networks around the world, including the NPR (Performance Today), Ireland's RTE, and Hong Kong's RTHK. He has also recorded the Sonatas of Scriabin and works of Beethoven, Schumann, Liszt, and Babbitt for Harmonia Mundi, several of which have been selected as "critic's favorites" by *Gramophone*, *Newsweek*, *The New York Times*, *The Washington Post*, *Ovation*, and *Fanfare*.

Robert Taub is involved with contemporary music as well as the established literature, premiering piano concertos by Milton Babbitt (MET Orchestra, James Levine) and Mel Powell (Los Angeles Philharmonic), and making the first recordings of the Persichetti Piano Concerto (Philadelphia Orchestra, Charles Dutoit) and Sessions Piano Concerto. He has premiered six works of Milton Babbitt (solo piano, chamber music, Second Piano Concerto). Taub has also collaborated with several 21st-century composers, including Jonathan Dawe (USA), David Bessell (UK), and Ludger Brümmer (Germany) performing their works in America and Europe.

Taub is a Phi Beta Kappa graduate of Princeton where he was a University Scholar. As a Danforth Fellow he completed his doctoral degree at The Juilliard School where he received the highest award in piano. Taub has served as Artist-in-Residence at Harvard University, at UC Davis, as well as at the Institute for Advanced Study. He has led music forums at Oxford and Cambridge Universities and The Juilliard School. Taub has also been Visiting Professor at Princeton University and at Kingston University (UK).